D1437074

STELLA ANDROMEDA

DOG
ASTROLOGY

DECODE YOUR PET'S PERSONALITY
WITH THE POWER OF THE ZODIAC

Hardie Grant

BOOKS

TO REX SCHWANKE. KING OF DOGS,
FAVOURITE AND FAITHFUL FRIEND.

INTRODUCTION

Just like us, every dog is born under an astrological sun sign which is determined by their date of birth. If you know the exact time and place of your dog's birth, you can even have their astrological birth chart drawn up which will yield even more information.

However, just knowing their sun sign will give you some insight into your dog's personality and character. This can then be helpful to your relationship and understanding how you might clash or chime with your pooch.

From Anubis, the ancient Egyptian god of the dead, to Charlie Brown's Snoopy; from the hound of the Baskervilles to Lord Byron's Boatswain who featured in his poetic dog epitaphs, from Lump the dachshund depicted by Picasso to Queen Elizabeth II's favourite corgi Susan, from Nipper the dog that immortalised His Master's Voice to Odysseus' faithful Argos, dogs have always featured in art, mythology, literature, commerce, culture and family life. And from Palaeolithic times to the annual UK dog show Crufts, dogs have always been considered man's prized and absolute best friend.

To his dog, every man is Napoleon; hence the constant popularity of dogs.

**ALDOUS HUXLEY,
WRITER AND AUTHOR**

CANIS LUPUS FAMILIARIS

The domesticated dog evolved from wolves; probably from the now extinct species of *canis lupus variabilis*. Palaeontologists working at the Gravettian Předmostí site in the Czech Republic in 2011 unearthed what appears to be the earliest evidence of the domestication of dogs in the Stone Age, and so dating back over 2 million years. They found the remains of three dogs – one of which had been buried with a bone believed to be that of a rhino, bison or even a mammoth – in its mouth.

Only a human being could have done this prior to burial, which suggests an emotional relationship of some sort with the dogs. That relationship has endured and continues to be of extreme importance in many people's lives.

Happiness is a warm puppy.

CHARLES SCHULZ,
AMERICAN CARTOONIST, AUTHOR OF *PEANUTS*

HOW CLEVER IS YOUR DOG?

You might think your dog is as daft as a brush, but according to scientists, dogs are super smart. 'If you look at wild wolves, they do not perform as well as domestic dogs. When a human points, the wolf will look at the finger, while the domestic dog will look where the finger is pointing,' says Professor Stanley Coren, a leading expert on canine intelligence at the University of British Columbia in Vancouver, who has researched the intelligence of domesticated dogs and, as a result, believes that centuries of selective breeding and living alongside humans has helped to hone their intelligence.

Researchers used tests originally designed to demonstrate the development of language, pre-language and basic arithmetic in children, and were able to show that the average dog is far more intelligent than they are sometimes given credit for. Dogs can understand about 165 words, signs and signals. Those in the top 20 per cent were able to understand as many as 250 words and signals, which is about the same as a two-year-old child.

Dogs do speak, but only to those who know how to listen.

ORHAN PAMUK,
NOBEL PRIZE FOR LITERATURE, 2006

BIG DOG CONSTELLATION

The brightest star visible from any part of Earth is Sirius in the constellation *Canis Major*, the Great Dog. Sirius is sometimes called the Dog Star and is most visible in the Northern Hemisphere during late summer, which has given rise to the saying, 'the dog days of summer'. Sirius can be seen at the heels of the constellation of Orion, the hunter, representing his faithful dog. In Egyptian mythology, Sirius is also associated with the god Osiris – god of death and regeneration.

FIRST DOG IN SPACE

Before Yuri Gagarin was the first man in space in 1961, a female terrier mix called Laika was the first cosmonaut dog, preceding him by four years into space in 1957 and orbiting the earth in the Russian satellite Sputnik 2.

While Laika's bravery captured the attention of the world's media, this soon turned to anger when it was revealed that there had been no provision made to return her safely to earth and tragically she died on re-entry to the earth's atmosphere.

LET SLEEPING DOGS LIE

This old saying advises us not to deliberately stir up trouble. It may originate from the Latin saying *Quieta non movere* which means do not move settled things and is also referenced in the 14th century *Proverbia Vulgalia et Latina* where it appears in French as '*Ne réveillez pas le chien qui dort*'.

This same idea also shows up in the Bible, in the Book of Proverbs [26:17] as, 'He that passes by and meddles with strife belonging not to him is like one that takes a dog by the ears.' And Chaucer used it in the 1380s in *Troilus and Criseyde* when he wrote, 'It is nought good a sleeping hound to wake.'

I myself have known some profoundly thoughtful dogs.

**JAMES THURBER,
CARTOONIST AND DOG LOVER**

DOGGIE DREAMS

If you've ever wondered whether your dog dreams when they're sleeping, science now suggests that they really do – which would explain all that twitching, whimpering and occasional woofing in their sleep!

Researchers have now tested canine brainwave activity during sleep using an electroencephalogram [EEG] and discovered dogs are actually very similar to humans when it comes to sleep patterns and brainwave activity.

Like us, dogs go through different sleep phases and when they enter a deep sleep stage, during which they have rapid eye movement [REM] then dreams occur, which is when they make those movements and noises that are a clue to the fun they are having while asleep.

What dogs are dreaming about – chasing rabbits, burying a bone, sniffing another dog's bottom – is anyone's guess, but they may move their legs as if running, pant with the excitement of the chase, whine or bark.

TRAIN YOUR DOG

While a dog might be man's best friend, they need to be socialised and learn obedience as pups so that everyone can live harmoniously and safely together. Attending a class with your dog can be helpful and fun but not essential as long as you are diligent and consistent about what your dog needs to learn. This includes teaching the basic command words: stay, sit, come.

You don't need to dominate your dog but it's important that they learn to respond to your command, and it is the responsibility of every dog owner to train their dog properly. Always reward good behaviour to reinforce it, rather than punishing errant behaviour, so they learn to trust you and want to please you.

Many dog breeds are well disposed to training and respond well to it and, with a reward in sight, are happy to conform. Always end a training session with lots of positive play and petting to show your pooch how much you love them.

BIRTH DATE

In an ideal world, you'd know the exact date, time and place of birth of your dog, but even just having their birth date will tell you which of the 12 zodiac signs they are. If you plan to get your dog from a breeder make a note to remember to ask them about the date and time of their birth.

However, if you have given your dog a forever home when they are less than newly born, it is unlikely you will have this information. In this case, you can take the date of their adoption into your life as the starting point of your relationship with them; it's just as meaningful.

And, of course, with a knowledge of each sun sign's astrological characteristics you will soon begin to fathom out some of those personality traits and be able to accurately identify their astrological star sign yourself.

AR

Aries

21 MARCH–20 APRIL

Aries is considered the first sign of the zodiac, and there's very much a 'me first' attitude about any dog born under this sign. They will want to rush off to explore with no fear of any of the consequences, so need to be thoroughly trained so you can bring them to heel when necessary and curb the worst of those headstrong characteristics. Luckily, Aries dogs are very quick to learn and also very loyal, so once they know you are the leader of their pack, they'll be happy to stay close and look to you for instruction.

One of the happiest signs of the Zodiac, an Aries dog loves adventure and so will want (and need) lots of walks interspersed with games like playing frisbee or fetching the stick or ball. Over and over again. You throw, they race and chase whatever you have thrown to return it and never seem to tire of the game.

Friendliness is the hallmark of this dog who wants to say hello to everyone and so, again, will need to be well trained to check first with you that it is OK to bowl over to welcome the new kid on the block, irrespective of whether they have four legs or two. Aries dogs are also intuitive and shrewd, so learn quickly and will respond well to you and your guidance.

Competitive to a fault, an Aries dog will always go that extra mile to be top dog and if you have several dogs is likely to be the leader of their particular pack. However independent an Aries dog appears to be, when it comes to loyalty, you can't beat them. Once committed to you, they are yours for life.

FIRE SIGN

DEPICTED BY

The Ram

RULED BY

The planet Mars

LUCKY DAY

Tuesday

WEAK SPOT

The head (and over-exertion)

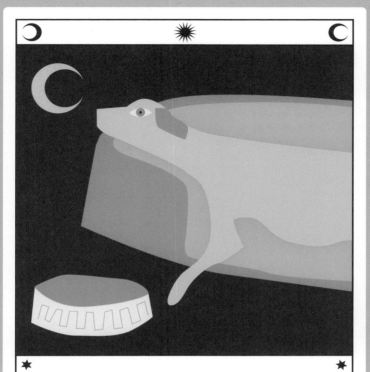

Temper that fire

Every dog needs to relax and none more so than a hyperactive Aries, so try to make sure your dog has plenty of downtime to compensate for all their extroversion and hyperactivity.

Working Aries dogs

This is a dog that has the brave temperament to train as a sniffer or bomb disposal dog, leading from the front but responsive to command. Hardworking, curious, intelligent and eager to please you, they understand how to get a job done.

Lucky colour

Your Aries dog's lucky colour is red, so when it comes to choosing a favourite blanket, collar, lead or other doggy accessory, choose red to reinforce you mutt's positive nature.

Aries names for dogs

Go for something short and sweet to match this active, inquisitive sign like Red (for the planet Mars), Will (for wilful), Scout (for their pioneering spirit) or even Aries or Ram.

Aries dog match

If you are also a fire sign you will have a similar energy to your Aries dog, while the gentle air sign Libra might calm things down. Gemini could overexcite, while Virgo's more grounded nature can provide balance.

Aries breed

Boisterous and affectionate, the Border Collie is a dog that likes to lead from the front and loves to herd. A high-energy breed with a low threshold for boredom, and thus typical of Aries, they thrive in big landscapes with plenty of exercise, love to be busy and hate to be curtailed.

RUS

Taurus

21 APRIL–20 MAY

Practical and compassionate by nature, Taurus dogs are among the most dependable and easy-going but they are also extremely tenacious. Not for them the easily-relinquished soft toy – they will hang on for dear life to something that has attracted their attention! This could also be your shoe or someone else's ball, so this trait needs to be carefully handled.

Train your Taurus by reward because this is the other side of this sun sign's nature – a susceptibility to tasty treats. In fact, they love their food (and yours too) so try to be strict about not overfeeding or feeding scraps from your plate because there's a tendency for Taurus dogs to overindulge and put on weight. And given their innate inclination to loaf about in clover rather than run wild through it, this is something to keep an eye on.

You might find your Taurus dog highly communicative, as this sun sign rules the throat. Loud barks, soft yips or gentle growls may all feature in your dog's more vocal repertoire, even when they are asleep.

Taurus dogs have a deep need for security, so you will be hard pushed to get them to share their bed or blanket with another. That blanket may also represent their security and they will retreat to it and their bed quite happily for some downtime. In fact, a Taurus dog is one of the most peaceful of all the signs and, since they enjoy proximity to others, will be more than happy to spend time snoozing at your feet or the end of your bed.

EARTH SIGN

DEPICTED BY

The Bull

RULED BY

The planet Venus

LUCKY DAY

Friday

WEAK SPOT

The neck, throat and sometimes the voice

Pamper that earth

This is a dog that is happy to take a bath and to be towelled dry, which is probably just as well as its earthy nature may mean that rolling in the dirt is another favourite pastime. Happily, this is also a pooch that loves to be groomed which plays to their sensuous nature.

Working Taurus dogs

Hardworking and team players by nature, happy to be stroked and delighted to keep someone company, a Taurus dog would make a good therapy dog, trained to provide comfort in nursing homes, retirement homes or hospices.

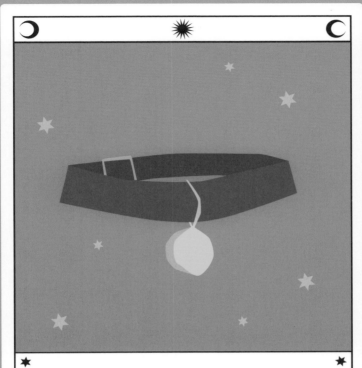

Lucky colour

Earthy greens and turquoise are your Taurus dog's lucky colours, so opt for a co-ordinating sensuous velvet collar, lead and other accessories within this colour range to play to their sun sign character.

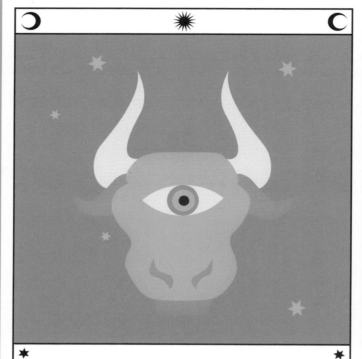

Taurus names

You could opt for the traditional name of the bull, Ferdinand, or any of its derivatives like Ferdi or Nando. Something earthy might suit, too, like Heath, Juniper, Huck (for Huckleberry) or Ash.

Taurus dog match

Taurus relates well to the other earth signs Virgo and Capricorn so this will be a harmonious relationship if you are one of these signs, while their opposite is watery Scorpio. An airy sign like Aquarius might put the wind up your earthy dog and fiery Leo's ego can be too much of a challenge.

Taurus breed

One of the more elegant versions of the Basset breed, the Grand Basset (aka the French *Griffon Vendéen*) has an affectionate but obstinate nature making the breed pure Taurean. A companionable breed, like many Taurus types they also enjoy having their thick coat groomed.

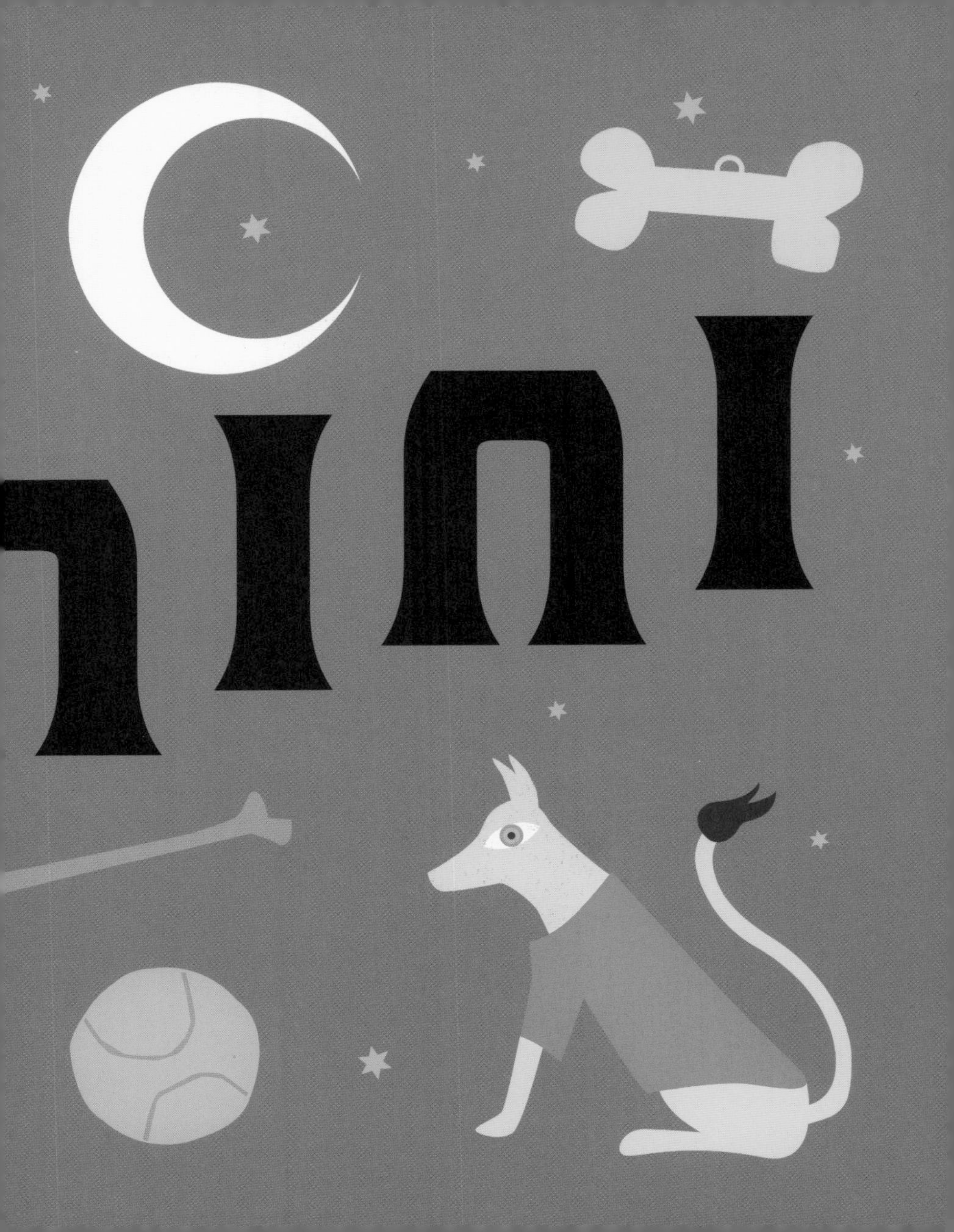

Gemini

Blessed with a lively disposition and ruled by Mercury (or Hermes in Greek mythology) who is depicted with winged heels, this is a dog that is fleet of foot and one that needs a lot of stimulation of both body and mind. Gemini dogs want and need to communicate so this is the dog in the park you're going to see endlessly engaging with other dogs and their owners. Gemini is also something of a flirt and so will happily communicate with anyone, from the postman to his pooch.

Training this lively dog will take some ingenuity and keeping them on task is not the easiest, because their butterfly brains tend to be easily distracted. Consistency will help, and also a regular daily routine, both of which will help instil a sense of order and an acceptance of who's 'boss' – that's you, the leader of their pack.

Easily over-stimulated – just sniffing the air can send a Gemini dog into a tailspin of excitement –and with a tendency towards hyperactivity, this is a dog that needs you to create relaxed moments for them to wind down and to provide a safe, familiar, quiet place or basket to do that. Get them into the habit of downtime from those first early days as a puppy by creating plenty of opportunities for quiet. They won't master this without your help!

There's a duality in Gemini represented by the twins, so they tend to be all-on or all-off – on the go one minute and zonked out the next. This is not a type that likes to idle in neutral.

AIR SIGN

DEPICTED BY

The Twins

RULED BY

The planet Mercury

LUCKY DAY

Wednesday

WEAK SPOT

The forelegs and shoulders

Gemini ♊

Temper that air

Easily over-excited and prone to rushing in where angels fear to tread, you will need to strike the right balance between making sure they have enough daily exercise to let off steam but also quiet time for grooming and relaxing, both of which will help soothe that airy nature.

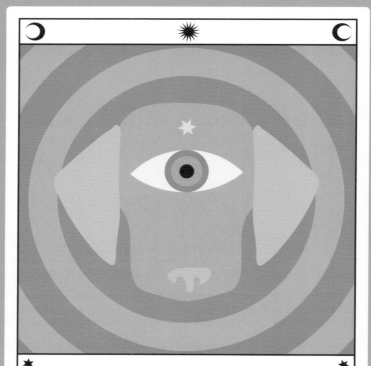

Working Gemini dogs

A willingness to interact and communicate makes Gemini dogs an excellent choice for a support dog for someone with epilepsy. Their amazing, quick-thinking minds make them ideal for the intense training that will teach them how to give an advance warning of seizures.

Lucky colour

Yellow in all its shades is Gemini's colour; bright, hopeful and used as a symbol of courage in Japan. Choose dog accessories in this sunny, cheerful colour for your Gemini hound.

Gemini names for dogs

When it comes to appropriate naming, you could go for the Gemini twins, Castor or Pollux, or think about calling them Hermes or Mercury after the god they are ruled by. Or choose a windy name like Mistral, Hooley or Sirocco to reflect that airy Gemini nature.

Gemini dog match

Geminis relate well to other air signs, so if that's you, there's already an affinity written in the stars. Choose a Gemini dog if you want to lift your watery spirit (Pisces, Cancer and Scorpio) but keep in mind that if you're a fire sign (Aries, Leo, Sagittarius) you may clash with your pup's airy temperament.

Gemini breed

With an aerodynamic body designed for speed, the Whippet epitomises the Gemini dog. They may look delicate and may need a yellow coat when it's chilly, but this breed is surprisingly robust (if a little thin-skinned). Affectionate and companionable, they make intelligent and lively pets with a gift for 'conversation'.

ceR

Cancer

21 JUNE–21 JULY

It's all about the feelings with Cancer. This is a dog that appears to read your mood and will respond to it, boosting your spirits when you're feeling a bit down and sharing your joys when you're up. If you get the impression that your pooch is really listening to you and can read you like a book, you'd be right. But don't mistake this dog for being dreamy; in spite of being ruled by the moon Cancer is a cardinal sign and there's a real strength running through their intuitive doggie soul that makes them highly dependable.

Tenacity is another Cancer trait that you may notice. You throw a ball, they happily fetch it, but then refuse to drop or give it back when asked. Or that toy they've had since they were a puppy? Right there in their basket, along with another ancient, favourite chew. Chuck it out at your peril! That same tenacity and ability to form strong attachments is what also makes them such a faithful friend, even if they have a crablike tendency to sidle up to you sideways instead of head on when you call them back to you.

This is also a dog that loves water – puddles, rivers, the sea – all of which will make them happy. Rest assured, they treat water with respect, caution even, and so won't take unnecessary risks, unless they have to rescue someone or something they love.

Finally, you can't mention Cancer without mentioning their maternal side and whatever their sex they are good at mothering. They may try to mother you, the children in the family, or other pets, and you will need to understand that strong nurturing instinct comes with the territory of the Cancer dog.

WATER SIGN

DEPICTED BY

The Crab

RULED BY

The Moon

LUCKY DAY

Monday

WEAK SPOT

The belly and digestive system

Calm those waters

All that emoting means that your Cancer dog can occasionally get a little overwrought and may sometimes need a gentle reminder that they are just a dog. Balance their lives with enough calm one-to-one moments to get back on track, through grooming or just sitting close and relaxing together, which they will love.

Working Cancer dogs

A dog that is smart, tenacious and loves to round up others to keep them safe? Sounds like the makings of an excellent sheepdog. A Cancerian hound will check up on each member of the family before they can settle themselves, just to make sure they're all present and correct and safe.

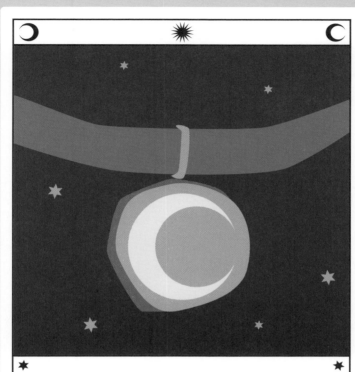

Lucky colour

Silver, like the light of the silvery moon, is Cancer's lucky colour – and also the silvery-blue green waves of the sea. These colours can make for some beautiful and stylish dog collars, coats and other accessories.

Cancer names for dogs

Acknowledge your Cancer dog's faithful devotion with the traditional and dependable name Fido, or, for a female, how about that famous domestic canine Nana from *Peter Pan*. Referencing their watery sign gives you Blue, Briny, Aqua or Marina.

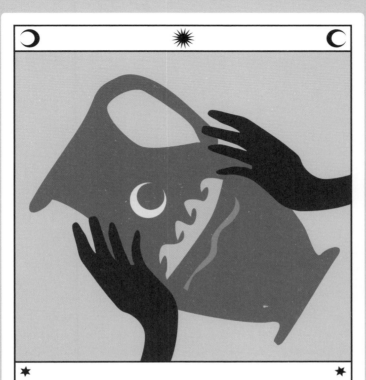

Cancer dog match

If you are also one of the water signs, you will understand your dog's watery inclinations and moods. Earthy Capricorn, which is Cancer's opposite sign, will help ground your pooch while fire signs can energise, although too much can create steam!

Cancer breed

Loving, loyal and gregarious by nature, the Labrador Retriever is, thanks to all its traits, one of the world's most popular dogs. They're also often water-lovers, a strong Cancer trait, and fisherman once relied on their strength to haul in fish-filled nets.

Leo

If your dog has a larger than life personality, is exuberant, outgoing and friendly in the extreme, chances are it's a Leo. There's something distinctly sunny about their personality, always up for a game, a walk or some soppy downtime with lots of ear ruffling. This is a dog that shows its love and devotion physically from the way it pricks up its ears as you turn the key in the front door when you come home, to the happy wagging of its tail when you're together. With this dog, loyalty to you comes as second nature.

Like the lion that depicts this sign, this is also a dog that believes it's the king of the jungle and often behaves like one. Whether your dog is a Chihuahua or a Great Dane even their bark is almost a roar, but always worse than their bite.

This is not a scrappy dog, up for a fight with anyone, just a mutt that thinks it's a monarch. With this streak of assumed royalty comes a huge demand for attention and while they give as much as they get, they will often be the first to ask for a reassuring stroke or nuzzle. One way to lavish this dog with the attention it thinks is its birthright is to brush them regularly. In fact, this sun sign dog loves to be groomed, because much like their human counterparts, Leos have a streak of vanity.

Leo dogs want to be recognised and applauded for everything they do, whether this is merely wagging their tail, retrieving a ball or performing some competitive feat. A show dog at heart, if you haven't given them any attention for a while, they will either nuzzle your hand or look reproachful until you do.

ಉ

Leo

DEPICTED BY

The Lion

RULED BY

The Sun

LUCKY DAY

Sunday

WEAK SPOT

The spine and the back in general

Leo ♌

Leo

Temper that fire

All that abundant energy can have its flipside, however, and this is a dog that can often over-indulge in everything from exercise to food, so they may need some help in letting go and chilling out. If they understand that their bed or kennel is their own personal castle, they will happily retreat there to recharge.

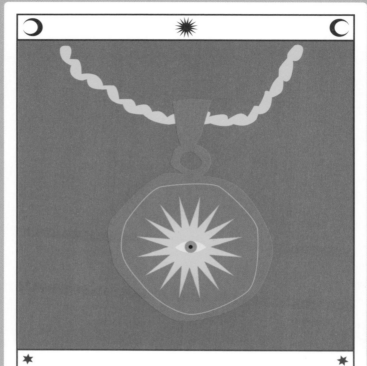

Working Leo dogs

A Leo's penchant for showing off may find them taking easily to learning new tricks. And, if they're the right breed and combine intelligence with a brave heart, they will work well alongside police and other law-enforcement personnel.

Lucky colour

Yellow, orange and regal gold are Leo's lucky colours, reflecting and boosting their energy. Choose these colours for their collar and other accessories to enhance their proud appearance and majesty.

Leo names

Anything regal suits this dog. King, Rex (which means 'king' in Latin), Prince, Regina or Queenie would all be a good name for the Leo dog. Alternatively, find a name that reflects a real life or fictional regal character like singer Elvis (often called the King), Argos (Ulysses' faithful dog), Simba, Cleopatra or Arthur.

Leo dog match

If you're also a fire sign like Aries, Sagittarius
or Leo, you'll be well matched with your Leo
dog. And if you are a water sign (Cancer, Scorpio,
Pisces), you may benefit from your dog's Leo
energy which will also bring extra power to you
if you're an air sign (Gemini, Libra, Aquarius).

Leo breed

Self-confident, active, strong and fun-loving, the Boxer has many of the key Leo characteristics. It can also look intimidating but, while its bark may be loud, it's a gentle breed by nature. Noble and proud in looks, Boxers are intelligent with fast reaction times, making them rewarding and lively companions.

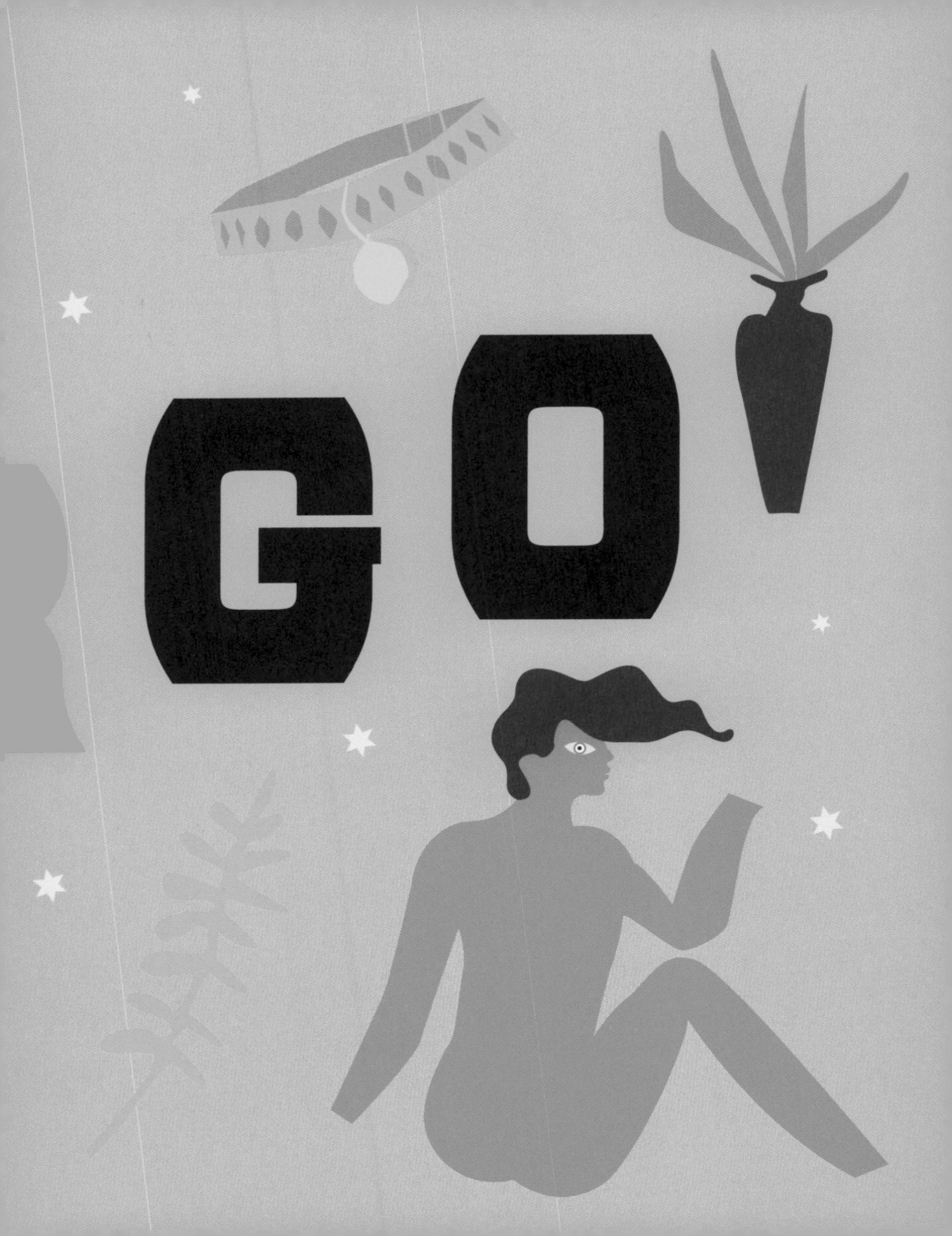
GO

Virgo

Traditionally considered the most fastidious of the sun signs, your Virgo dog may surprise you with their fussiness about the freshness of their water bowl, or the tidiness of their basket. This is a pooch that may reject a dirty plate where another wouldn't notice, and they will take great exception to another pet trying to share their food. It's not unfriendliness, just a desire to have their own space respected.

Virgos are noted for their reserve and they need to know what's what, where everything is and who's in charge. With a tendency to worry and fret if things aren't quite as they expect, your Virgo dog will find routine reassuring and will be happiest when their bowl is not only in its proper place but filled at a regular time – in fact, you could probably set your watch around their feed times. As long as there's some regularity and routine to their day, your Virgo dog can relax and enjoy just being a dog.

A regular routine is what lies at the heart of a happy relationship with this mutt and once you've cracked that secret, the rest will come more easily. Every pup needs to feel secure so don't misinterpret this as being demanding or excessively needy, because once they are properly settled with you, they will become more independent and outgoing. Just remember to give your Virgo dog a little extra time to adapt to anything new. And remember that spontaneity isn't one of their virtues.

♍

Virgo

DEPICTED BY

The Corn Maiden

RULED BY

The planet Mercury

LUCKY DAY

Wednesday

WEAK SPOT

The nervous system and the gut, which are often interrelated

♍

Virgo

Pamper that earth

Those Virgo instincts for routine and reliability are very strong, but there's a strongly sensual streak, too, characteristic of all earth signs. Your dog may sometimes seem a little aloof, but he or she will need as much love and attention as those dogs that demand it constantly.

♍

Virgo

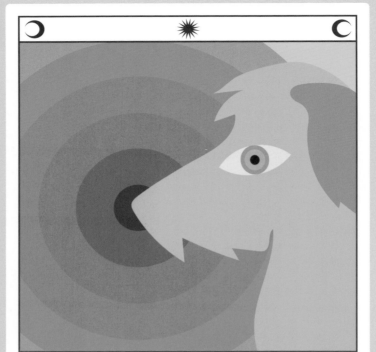

Working Virgo dogs

Your Virgo dog is unlikely to miss a trick and, once trained, could use their sense of smell to become a wonderful detection or sniffer dog. Their attention to detail can help them learn to sniff out explosives, illegal drugs, contraband mobile phones and other items that need detection in places like prisons.

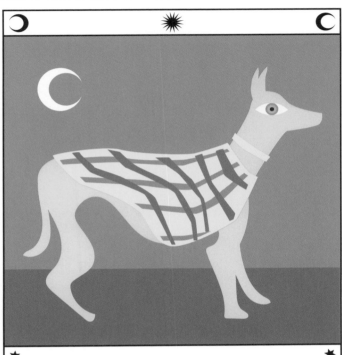

Lucky colour

Shades of blue from pale to navy reflect this sun sign's methodical energy but still allow plenty of scope for variety in a chequered coat or striped collar. This is a colour range with lots of choice for the daintiest to the most dramatic of Virgo hounds.

Virgo names

Choose something that reflects your Virgo dog's earthy but beautiful nature like Artemis (virgin goddess), Freya (of the earth) or Terre (earth), or perhaps choose a name related to industriousness and hard work, like Galen, Thane or Emil.

Virgo dog match

Well matched with earth signs (Virgo, Capricorn or Taurus), a Virgo dog can also bring some grounding to airy or water sign owners like Gemini, Aquarius or Pisces: it's all about balancing the energy between you and them.

Virgo breed

Known colloquially as sausage dogs, or 'earth dogs' (as befits an earth sign), the Dachshund originated in Germany, but similar looking dogs also appear in ancient Egyptian art. Originally bred for work, with their bright, intelligent faces, they have become a hugely popular and much-loved domestic dog.

LIB

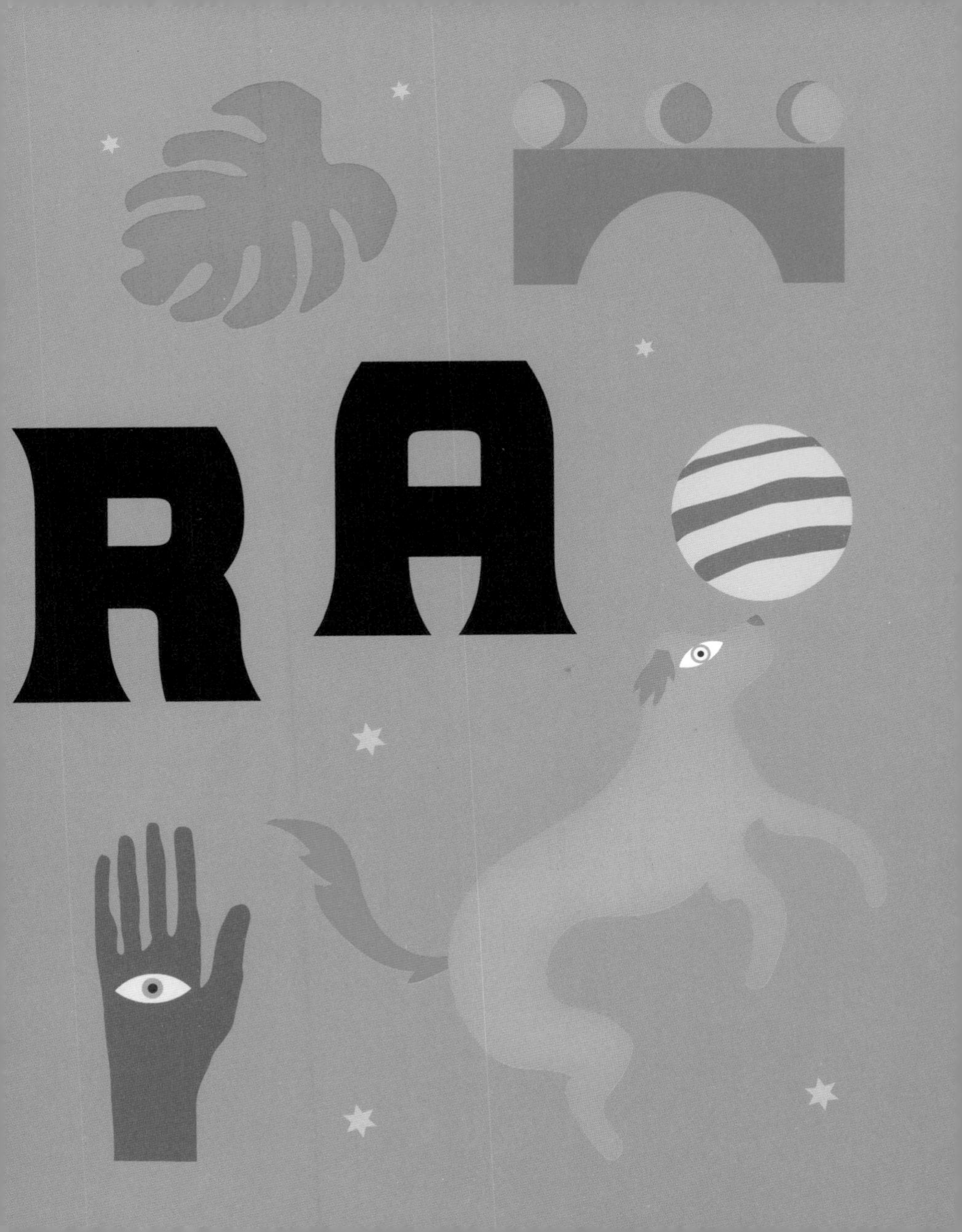
RA

Libra

The scales are all about balance and striving for this is a key feature of Libra personality, so this is a dog that likes to keep the peace in his human family, welcomes harmony and tries to please you. This is not a dog to pick an unnecessary fight or go looking for trouble. But underneath this rather cautious exterior runs an airy energy and a natural friendliness making them an easy and companionable pet.

Relationships are very important to this sign and so you may find your Libran dog buddying up to another pet or, in the absence of that, partnering up with you. They'll also notice if you favour one pet over another, so be sure you're giving equal attention to them and any other pet.

By and large you're looking at a personality type that strives for balance, but the other side of this can be indecision. Is your dog always on the wrong side of the door, never sure if they want to be in... or out? Do they want to be petted... or left alone? That's typical of Libra. Spending time trying to weigh up the pros and cons, rather than just going with their heart.

Ruled by the goddess of love and beauty, Venus also gives this dog an inclination for the finer things in life which can extend to the food they'll eat or the quality of their basket. And they're disinclined to tolerate a messy basket either, discarding ancient chewed-up favourites amongst their toys the minute their attraction has passed. There's definitely a touch of disdain for the commoner things in life – this is a pooch who loves and needs to be pampered.

Libra

DEPICTED BY

The Scales

RULED BY

The planet Venus

LUCKY DAY

Friday

WEAK SPOT

The kidneys and lower, sacral area of the back

Libra

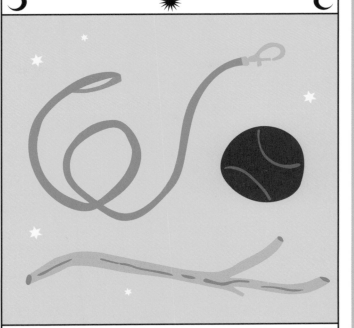

Calm that air

Prone to feelings of uncertainty, it's important for Libra dogs to ground themselves in more physical ways. Help them to do this by ensuring that exercise and grooming are routinely part of their day. This helps them strengthen a sense of connection to their bodies, and calms them down when stressed.

Libra

Working Libra dogs

These are bright, often physically graceful dogs
capable of being trained and having the sort of
self-reliance and sociability that makes them
excellent seeing-eye dogs. Responsive and quick
to learn, they are alert to command and love to
work in a harmonious partnership.

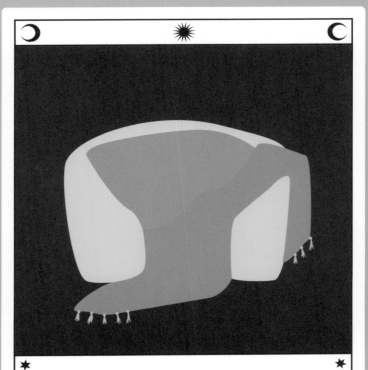

Lucky colour

Cool shades of blue, particularly pastel tones
that reflect the air, appeal to a Libra soul that
likes harmony and calm. Choose these hues for
their blanket and to create security in their basket
or sleeping area.

Libra names

Harmony is one, while Cosima and Concordia have similar meanings in Greek and Roman myth, as does the name Kazuki in Japanese. Dan means 'he judged' in Hebrew, Dempster is Old English for 'judge', and Oliver means 'peace'. And, of course, there's Libra, or Libby.

Libra dog match

There's an affinity with other air signs Aquarius
and Gemini, but also a need for grounding
so if you are an earth sign like Taurus, Virgo
or Capricorn, that would work well, too.

Libra breed

Beauty, grace and intelligence make the gorgeous Afghan dog the epitome of a Libran dog breed. Once seen as the archetypal fashion accessory – their long coat makes daily grooming essential – this coat originally served a particular purpose, providing protection against the cold of the mountains of Afghanistan.

Libra

Scorpio

22 OCTOBER–21 NOVEMBER

Still waters run deep and Scorpios are renowned for their deep-seated loyalty to their tribe and those they love. That sting in their tail, characteristic of the scorpion? With your Scorpio dog this simply means they are super protective of those they love and can react strongly to any perceived threat. They may also become a tad jealous if you give too much attention elsewhere! That said, Scorpios have a deeply intuitive streak, so if you think your pup is watching you closely – and even sizing you up – they probably are.

This is also a pet with a secretive streak, so if things go missing or get hidden or buried, this is just a part of their Scorpio trait. Even their favourite toy could get hidden away and they may guard their possessions quite fiercely if they feel they're at risk. Hide and seek will be a game they will want to play over and over again, as will chasing and retrieving the ball. And in between times, the Scorpio dog will often be quite content with their own company and solitude.

For all their quirky ways, a Scorpio dog is not without many positive virtues and will surprise you with their sensitivity to your mood. Don't think they won't notice if you've had a hard day, they will and will want to make it up to you by showing allegiance and companionship. You may have read, too, that Scorpios are a sensual sign, and this gets expressed in their need to give and receive attention. They also have a deep inner streak of calm and will be as happy to sit quietly close-by as walking with you in the park.

WATER SIGN

DEPICTED BY

The Scorpion

RULED BY

The planet Pluto

LUCKY DAY

Tuesday

WEAK SPOT

The reproductive organs, in both the male and female

Calm that water

Emotions run deep in water signs and you may be struck by just how sensitive your dog can be and in need of reassurance. Needing to stay close to you or under the bed in a thunderstorm, for example, would be a very Scorpio trait.

Working Scorpio dogs

Because they thrive in one-to-one relationships and are sensitive and loyal, your Scorpio dog has the makings of a reliable medical assistance dog, trained to support people with complex health conditions like diabetes and other endocrine disorders.

Lucky colour

Deep reds and purples resonate with the passionate energy of Scorpio and make bold and stylish accessories. These shades can also create a secure, womb-like feel to their rug or dog basket where they can find restorative solitude.

Scorpio names

Names that mean 'secret' would fit, making Cabal, Kasper, Rune, Humraz or Raz contenders. Something like Trix or Trixie, Ananzi or Puck might reflect their quixotic nature, while names with watery connotations like Brook, Darya, Gully or Eddy might work.

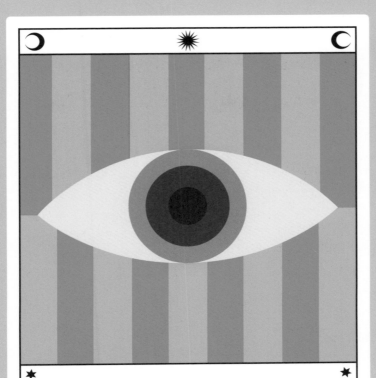

Scorpio dog match

Similar water signs Cancer and Pisces understand the highly emotional side of Scorpio, but if you are an air sign like Aquarius, Gemini and Libra, this can sometimes help to lighten the intensity of the Scorpio dog mood.

Scorpio breed

The Airedale terrier shows numerous Scorpio characteristics, including a stubborn streak and a need for mental stimulation that isn't immediately obvious. With lots of positive training to manage their quirky nature, this terrier is typical of a loyal and rewarding Scorpio.

Sagittarius

The sign of Sagittarius is depicted by a centaur – half-man half-horse – equipped with a bow and arrow which depicts this sign's urge to fire off in a forward direction, always seeking adventure. That a Sagittarius dog is fleet of foot will be an understatement! They are always looking beyond the horizon and keen to set off on a journey to reach it. This is one of the most adventurous of signs and your dog is likely to show every indication of wanting to run wild and free.

Luckily, this is also a sign that loves company, and especially the company of those they love, so however far they like to wander, they will always return home. In fact, snoozing on the hearth, literally or metaphorically, is another favourite pastime of this fire sign, which needs to recharge its batteries once the adventuring is done. So, while out of sight tends to mean out of mind for this dog, they also need their creature comforts to revive their energy and however far they venture, will always find their way back to you.

This freedom-loving type isn't your traditional lapdog, though. They won't take kindly to being kept indoors and will want to take *you* for a walk each day, even if this is just around their patch rather than the great wild yonder. If you enjoy hiking and camping and the Great Outdoors, then a Sagittarius dog will be your faithful companion and guide because exploring the next horizon is second nature to this hound.

♐

Sagittarius

FIRE SIGN

DEPICTED BY

The Centaur

RULED BY

The planet Jupiter

LUCKY DAY

Thursday

WEAK SPOT

The legs, particularly the hip joints

Temper that fire

All that energy and adventure needs some downtime and a reminder to eat and drink regularly. Luckily this fire sign also appreciates a peaceful hearth, to which they willingly return between escapades.

Working Sagittarius dogs

Sagittarius can make a great sheepdog as they are intelligent, intuitive, respond to instruction and enjoy working in partnership. They also love working outdoors and, as long as they are the top-dog they're happy – which, with a flock of sheep to corral, they will be!

Lucky colour

Purple, the colour of clerics and philosophers, is lucky for Sagittarius. Whether this is a deep vibrant mulberry or a pale lilac hue, there is something within this range to suit all tastes from collars and leads to coats.

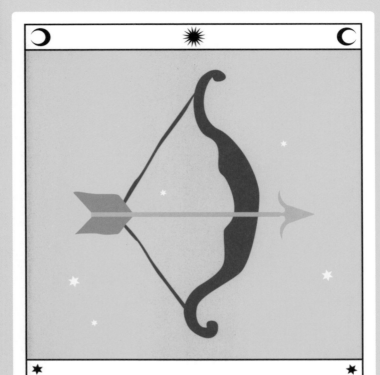

Sagittarius names

Anything that chimes with Sagittarian traits might include Archie (for archer), Hunter, Rover or Scout. Or perhaps an explorer – Christopher Columbus, Gertrude Bell, Thor Heyerdahl, Ferdinand Magellan, Scott (of the Antarctic), Sacagawea, Marco Polo, Darwin or Millie (Amelia Earhart).

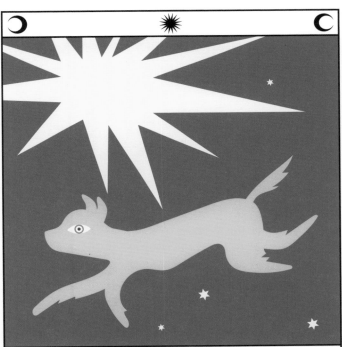

Sagittarius dog match

Similarly adventurous types like Aries and Leo would enjoy a Sagittarian dog for a pet, while those more homebound sun signs like Cancer and Virgo might benefit from a er pull in a more outgoing and energetic direction.

Sagittarius breed

Once only allowed to be owned by Scottish nobility, there's a grace to a Deerhound that resonates with Sagittarius and makes this a good-natured, outgoing and companionable breed for life's journeys.

Capricorn

22 DECEMBER–20 JANUARY

If your dog seems to take life rather seriously and is sometimes a little withdrawn, bear in mind that every Capricorn has a realistic streak a mile wide, so when you say it's time for a walk, they'll probably do little more than cock an ear until they're 100 per cent sure you mean it.

This is not a dog you can fool as they have an earthy intelligence rooted in the factual not the fictional. This is a pooch that is looking just as closely at what you do, as much as what you say.

Reliability tends to be Capricorn's middle name, too, but don't think this is boring, because a reliable dog is one to be truly appreciated, especially if your pet is a working asset or lives in a family with children. And where another dog might fret and pester you for its meals, if you're busy on a task then this is a canine with the class to wait its turn.

Patience is another trait of this earth sign, even if this means gently dogging your footsteps to get the attention they need and, like every other earth sign, they will need to be petted regularly and reassured of your love.

The Capricorn dog is also blessed with an earthy, sensual streak. And for all their apparent self-reliance, this is not a dog with an aloof character. Their good nature makes them easy to live with and once they are committed to you, then it's for life.

EARTH SIGN

DEPICTED BY

The Mountain Goat

RULED BY

The planet Saturn

LUCKY DAY

Saturday

WEAK SPOT

The joints and a susceptibility to arthritis

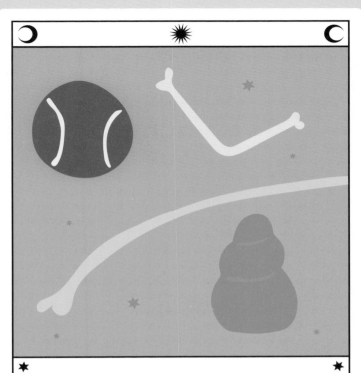

Pamper that earth

Capricorn can sometimes get a little bogged
down when the terrain is rough and can take life
rather seriously, so be sure to lighten their load
from time to time with games and fun pastimes.
Remind your Capricorn dog that it's important
to occasionally stop to smell the roses, and let the
wind lift their spirits and ruffle their fur.

Working Capricorn dogs

This dog is a real grafter, easy to train and keen to please with a diligence that makes them suitable for working with the blind or partially sighted. Their sense of responsibility also comes into play here, as Capricorns never like to let anyone down.

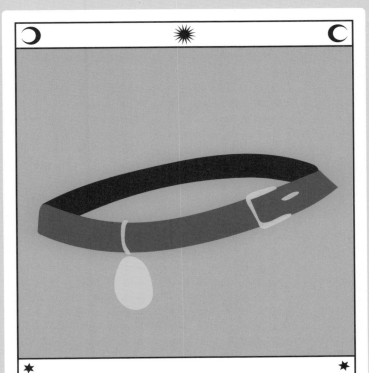

Lucky colour

Tones of earthy brown and dark green, firmly rooted in the everyday, are Capricorn's lucky colours. Choose your pet's accessories from within this range which will give them a psychological lift.

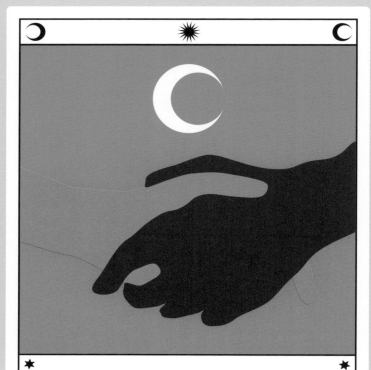

Capricorn names

You may not want to call your dog Goat, but Billy might work? Along with Nanny. Otherwise, go for a depiction of friendship with Buddy, Amigo, Buster, Mate or Mario.

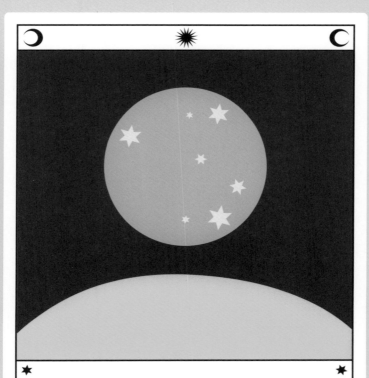

Capricorn dog match

If you are an earth sign too, you'll understand your Capricorn dog better than most, but a fire sign like Sagittarius can work well to energise this dog, while an air sign like Aquarius will help open up their view of the world.

Capricorn breed

Like Capricorn, the Pyrenean Sheepdog is a hardworking breed known for its mountain affinity. Small and agile it was bred to herd and guard sheep from mountain wolves, its warm coat making it suitable for harsh weather. Biddable in nature and relatively small in size, this dog makes a happy domestic pet, too.

AQUA

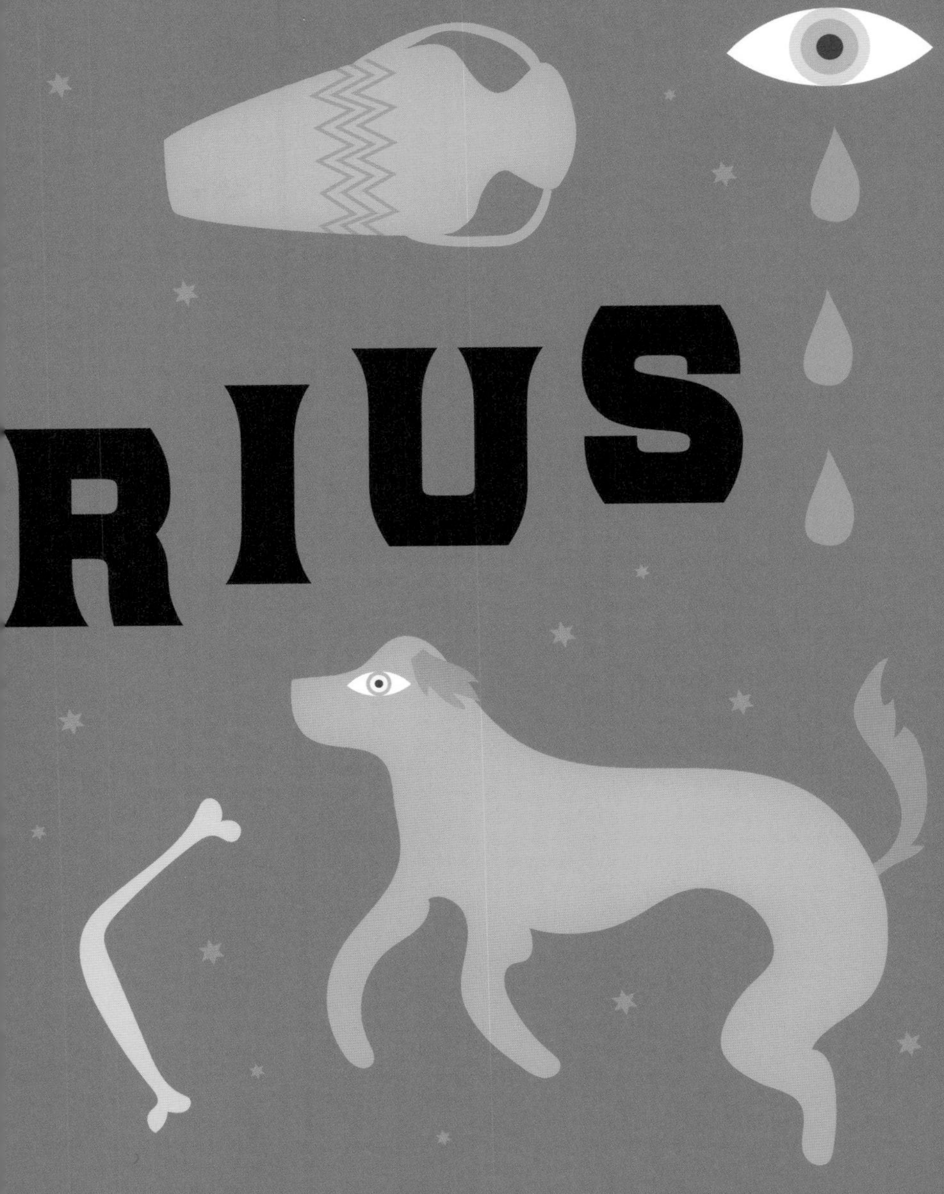
RIUS

Aquarius

Aquarius is all about freedom and independence and so however well trained your dog may be, you may notice an inclination to challenge the *status quo* from time to time, so make sure your mutt is microchipped in case they wander. Sometimes you may wonder exactly who is taking whom for a walk, but that's the price you pay for a smart dog and this one is also savvy about getting what he wants by working with you rather than against you.

Outright rebellion isn't written in this pooch's stars, although they can come close, but they are usually canny enough to fit in with you because they know it's in their own best interest.

That inclination to work as part of a team is another feature of this air sign, although having their head in the clouds is a big part of the way they see the world. They seem to 'get' the big ideas and have the tolerance to wait things out. So that lovely ramble through the woods that needs a 20-minute car journey to get there? They've understood that's part of what it takes and are prepared to 'go with the flow' like the water carrier they depict.

People will often remark of an Aquarius dog, 'What a character!' because their distinctive approach to life often sets them apart from the rest of the pack. This sun sign has a natural interest in people, places and things and has an instinct for novelty, which means they will always be happy to accompany you and share new experiences.

Aquarius

DEPICTED BY

The Water Carrier

RULED BY

The planet Uranus

Aquarius

LUCKY DAY

Wednesday

WEAK SPOT

The circulation, blood and lymphatic system

Temper that air

All that airy independence can sometimes need grounding and so your dog will need regular physical interaction to stay on an even keel. Although they might not be wild about bathing – too wet! – grooming, petting and hugs all help give Aquarius dogs a bit of balance.

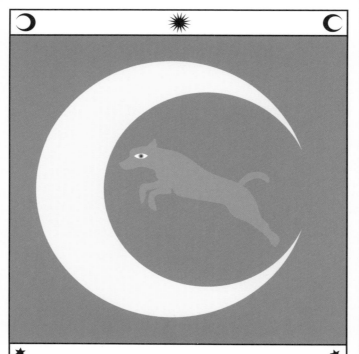

Working Aquarius dogs

The first dog in space, Laika, could have been an Aquarius; individual, independent and sent off to experience the most airiest place imaginable. Being the team leader of sleigh dogs, like the Chinook on the Antarctic expeditions in the 1920s, might suit an Aquarius dog with their inclination to explore.

Lucky colour

Blue. The blue of the sky in all its changing hues is lucky for this air sign. From the indigo of the dusk to the sky-blue pink of the dawn, whatever your dog's colouring there's a shade of blue to bring them luck, whether this is a collar or rug, or their bed of dreams.

Aquarius

Aquarius names

Names that are reminiscent of the air could work well – Airy, Breezy or Puff, while Sky, Celeste and Aurora are more romantically inclined. Perhaps Zephyr, Sirocco, Mistral or Hurricane, or simply Blue for their lucky colour.

Aquarius dog match

Other air signs will relate, but a better match
in an owner might be an earth sign like Taurus
or Virgo, to help ground all that airiness, while
Sagittarius will understand the desire for
freedom. Water signs like Cancer often provide
the nurture needed, too.

Aquarius breed

The Irish Setter loves to run wild with the wind in its fur and requires a lot of daily exercise to calm its nature. While it has an independent streak, it's a dog loyal to humanity, much like Aquarius itself, and responds well to training having been originally bred as a gun dog.

Aquarius

ces

Pisces

If you have a dog that twitches and woofs in their sleep, chances are their dream world is pretty active and this is typical of Pisces, who lives life somewhere between the real world and that of their imagination. In fact, this sign is often a bit dreamy and just as comfortable in their own internal world, as well as the external one, moving easily between them like the two fish swimming in opposite directions that depict this sign.

Intuitive and emotionally aware, this is also a dog that will pick up on your moods, whether happy or sad, often reflecting these in their own behaviour. Even if you're just shedding a tear at a weepie movie, your pet will look concerned and offer a nudge with its nose in support, almost as if they have a second sense, sensitive to the atmosphere around them.

Pisces is often considered to be the sign of the actor and your canny canine may be 'acting out' what you're feeling. And it's true, at times your Pisces pet will seem to function on a spiritual level, picking up on extra-sensory perceptual vibes like no other.

Managing strong emotions can make your pooch a tad insecure and while Pisces is by nature friendly, they sometimes play the shy card and will look to you for reassurance, especially if unsure of their environment. But this is also the most playful of signs and playing with you, other pets or even alone with their favourite toy will be one of their great joys.

♓

Pisces

WATER SIGN

DEPICTED BY

Two Fish

RULED BY

The planet Neptune

LUCKY DAY

Friday

WEAK SPOT

The feet, so may be liable to foot problems

Calming the waters

Help your dog balance all that watery emotion with a gentle and gradual exposure to new experiences and build lots of physical play into their day, which will also help to ground them. Good training and learning by example in puppy classes when they're young will further help them become a little more robust, too.

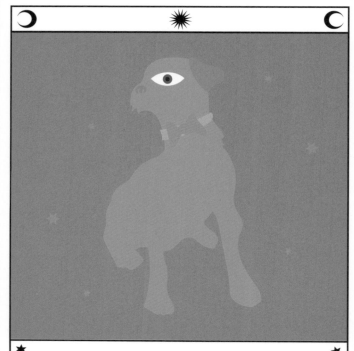

Working Pisces dogs

One of the most adaptable of signs, your Pisces dog can learn and adapt to many roles. They may also have creative side and an inclination towards performing and learning the skills needed for acting roles, like Uggie the Parson Jack Russell terrier in the movie *The Artist*.

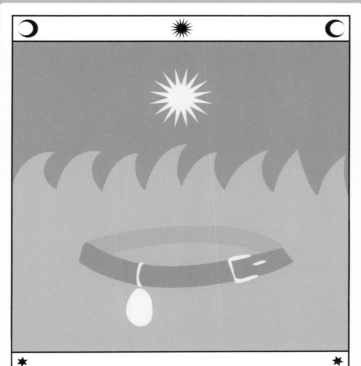

Lucky colour

The blue/green of the sea is Pisces' lucky colour and moving through this spectrum from a silvery glint to an oceanic dark navy depth will give you lots of scope for your pet's accessories to enhance and promote their dreamy side.

Pisces names

A water deity like Neptune is a big name for
a dog, while other watery names include Nerida,
Beck and Gill (stream), Arroyo (Spanish for
'deep gully'), Bayou, Brooklyn, Hamako (child
of the shore), Moses or Ula; there are just so
many beautiful possibilities for this dreamy dog.

Pisces dog match

Fellow water signs Cancer and Scorpio might bring out the worst in each other, whereas an air sign like Libra or Gemini will help lighten the mood. A strong earth sign owner, like Capricorn, will bring a nice balance to the relationship between dog and owner.

Pisces breed

Portuguese Water dogs are an ancient breed, strong and loyal, and also known as Cão de Agua. Agile swimmers, they were used in the past by fishermen to haul nets. This is the breed President Obama chose for the family dog Bo, because its coat is hypoallergenic.

About the Author

Stella Andromeda has been studying astrology for over 30 years, believing that a knowledge of the constellations of the skies and an understanding of their potential for psychological interpretation can be a useful tool. This extension of her study into book form makes modern insights about the ancient wisdom of the stars easily accessible and shares her passionate belief that reflection and self-knowledge can only empower us in life. With her sun in Taurus, Aquarius ascendant and moon in Cancer, she utilises earth, air and water to inspire her own astrological journey.

Acknowledgements

Particular thanks are due to Kate Pollard,
Publishing Director at Hardie Grant, for her
Taurean passion for beautiful books and
for commissioning this series. And to
editor Eila Purvis, for all her hard work and
attention to detail. While the illustrations
and design talent of Evi O Studio have
produced small works of art. With such
a star-studded team, these books can
only shine and for that, my thanks.

Published in 2021 by Hardie Grant Books,
an imprint of Hardie Grant Publishing

Hardie Grant Books (London)
5th & 6th Floors
52–54 Southwark Street
London SE1 1UN

Hardie Grant Books (Melbourne)
Building 1, 658 Church Street
Richmond, Victoria 3121

hardiegrantbooks.com

British Library Cataloguing-in-Publication Data. A catalogue record for this
book is available from the British Library.

Dog Astrology
ISBN: 978-1-78488-388-1

10 9 8 7 6 5 4 3 2 1

Publisher: Kajal Mistry
Editor: Eila Purvis
Design and Illustrations: Evi-O.Studio
Copyeditor: Susan Clark
Production Controller: Katie Jarvis

Colour reproduction by p2d
Printed and bound in China by Leo Paper Products Ltd.